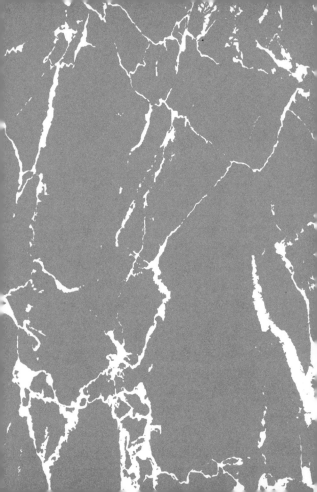

PROSECCO

is always the

ANSWER

summersdale

An Hachette UK Company
www.hachette.co.uk

Summersdale Publishers Ltd
Part of Octopus Publishing Group Limited
Carmelite House
50 Victoria Embankment
LONDON
EC4Y 0DZ
UK

www.summersdale.com

Printed and bound in the Czech Republic

ISBN: 978-1-78685-496-4

Substantial discounts on bulk quantities of Summersdale books are available to corporations, professional associations and other organisations. For details contact general enquiries: telephone: +44 (0) 1243 771107 or email: enquiries@summersdale.com.

TO..

FROM..

WHAT IS PROSECCO?

Prosecco is a crisp, refreshing Italian sparkling wine that has taken the world by storm recently. With over 475 million bottles now produced in Italy every year, the popularity of this bubbly shows no signs of slowing.

Prosecco now competes with its pricey French counterpart, champagne, for the accolade of being the world's favourite sparkling wine. Due to our ever-increasing thirst for it, we have even been threatened with global shortages, as producers have struggled to keep up with demand! So why is Prosecco so popular?

Firstly, this fizz is good value, making it a more affordable everyday luxury. It's also easy to drink, thanks to its light and fruity taste, and very versatile. It can be enjoyed whenever the mood strikes, but still has a touch of luxury, making it the perfect tipple to accompany a relaxed night in or a social celebration.

THE DIFFERENCE BETWEEN PROSECCO AND CHAMPAGNE

- Prosecco might be on a par with champagne when it comes to popularity, but these days annual production of it is higher than the famous French fizz.

- Both bubblies are classed as sparkling wines - they are simply produced in different countries.

- The pressure inside a bottle of Prosecco is 2-4 atm (atmospheric pressure), compared to the 6-7 atm of champagne. The lower pressure of Prosecco is due to its production method that involves having the second fermentation in tanks, while champagne is fermented inside the same bottle it is served from.

- Because of its different method of fermentation, Prosecco is easier to make, so less expensive than champagne.

- Due to its closer contact with yeast, champagne has more autolytic flavours – think bread, brioche and toast – as well as delicate citrus flavours. Prosecco, however, is more about fruity flavours: pear and apple, as well as honeysuckle and floral notes.

- Generally, Prosecco's bubbles last longer than beer's but not as long as champagne's.

- Prosecco does not improve over time like champagne, and should be drunk within three years of production.

THE HISTORY OF PROSECCO

- Prosecco was first produced as far back as Roman times, using the Glera grape, which initially grew near the village of Prosecco in the hills above Trieste, formerly known as Puccino.

- In the eighteenth century, cultivation of Glera grapes expanded throughout the hills of Veneto and Friuli. It is still widely believed that the best Prosecco is produced in these regions.

- These regions are also where the fizz we know today - using the modern fermentation method - was first produced at the beginning of the twentieth century.

- Prosecco is the main ingredient of the famous Bellini cocktail, created in Harry's Bar in Venice in the 1930s, and has historically been a key ingredient of Spritz, a style of cocktail popular in northern Italy.

KNOWING YOUR
VARIETIES AND GRAPES

Not all Prosecco is bubbly. The one we know best is called *spumante* (meaning sparkling wine), but there are also *frizzante* (semi-sparkling) and *tranquillo* (still) varieties.

There are four categories of Prosecco: brut, extra-dry, dry and demi-sec, which range from driest to sweetest, respectively. Brut styles of Prosecco are perfect paired with foods such as air-dried ham, sushi or mild cheeses. Sweeter styles of Prosecco work well with light sponge cakes, Italian biscuits or macarons.

The average alcohol content of Prosecco is 11–12 per cent, so it is considered a light wine. Typically, it should have fruity notes of yellow apple, pear, white peach and apricot, and a simple taste based on primary aromas.

Although Prosecco was originally made solely from the Glera grape, these days it can also be made with other varieties (up to 15 per cent of the total), including Chardonnay, Pinot Grigio, and even Pinot Noir.

Genuine Prosecco can be identified by the Denominazione di Origine Controllata (DOC) stamp that is usually on the bottles' labels. The stamp indicates that strict rules governing quality and geographical authenticity have been followed.

PROSECCO FOR EVERYONE

Prosecco is so popular there's now a National Prosecco Day in the UK each year on 13 August. Today, you're never far away from everyone's favourite fizz – you can find it at Prosecco festivals, bars, temporary pop-ups and even in shopping centres, but you don't even have to drink it to enjoy its sparkling beauty. It's so popular it can now be found in soaps, lip balms, bath bombs, scented candles, chocolates and sweets, as well as some of our favourite dishes.

If you prefer to savour its delights as a drink, but want to mix things up a little, then you can find in this book some sensational cocktail recipes to pimp your Prosecco.

PROSECCO ESSENTIALS

Here is a list of essential items you will need when making the Prosecco cocktails in this book:

- Champagne flute
- Martini glass
- Wine glass
- Tumbler
- Collins glass
- Cocktail shaker
- Blender
- Jug
- Punch bowl
- Jigger
- Measuring spoons

FROZEN LEMON FIZZER

SERVES 2

A fresh and citrusy pick-me-up,
perfect for the summer months.

INGREDIENTS

* 4 scoops lemon sorbet
  (home-made or shop-bought)

* 50 ml limoncello

* 60 ml Prosecco

* 2 sprigs fresh mint

METHOD

* Blend the lemon sorbet on a low speed and
  add the limoncello slowly.

* Add the Prosecco.

* Pour into chilled cocktail glasses and serve
  garnished with mint.

PENICILLIN CURES,
BUT WINE MAKES
PEOPLE HAPPY.

ALEXANDER FLEMING

I MAKE
PROSECCO
DISAPPEAR.

*What's your
superpower?*

SOBRIETY DIMINISHES,
DISCRIMINATES AND
SAYS NO; DRUNKENNESS
EXPANDS, UNITES
AND SAYS YES.

WILLIAM JAMES

PROSECCO AND MIXED BERRY JELLIES

SERVES 6

It's guaranteed that this fizzy
and fruity explosion of flavours
will make you feel fabulous!

INGREDIENTS

- 135 g raspberry jelly

- 475 ml Prosecco

- 200 g mixed summer berries, such as
  strawberries, raspberries, blackcurrants and
  blackberries, hulled and halved if necessary

- 142 ml carton single cream, to serve

- Fresh mint leaves, to decorate

METHOD

- Pour 100 ml of boiling water over the jelly cubes and stir until the jelly has dissolved. Let it cool, then slowly stir in the Prosecco.

- Divide the fruit between six Martini or wine glasses, then pour some of the jelly into each, to just cover the fruit. Wrap the tops of the glasses with cling film and chill for a couple of hours until the surface is just set.

- Top up with the remaining jelly, cover and chill until set.

- Pour a thin layer of cream onto each jelly, then decorate with fresh mint leaves.

HERE'S TO ALCOHOL, THE ROSE-COLOURED GLASSES OF LIFE.

F. SCOTT FITZGERALD

WITHOUT BREAD AND WINE, LOVE GOES HUNGRY.

PROVERB

CLASSIC BELLINI

SERVES 4

The famous Bellini was invented in
1934 by Giuseppe Cipriani, founder
of Harry's Bar in Venice.

INGREDIENTS

* 2 ripe peaches (peeled, halved and
  stones removed) or the equivalent using
  tinned peaches in their natural juice

* 1 bottle chilled Prosecco

METHOD

- Place the peaches in a blender and puree until totally smooth. Spoon half into four chilled champagne flutes and slowly top up with Prosecco, stirring as you pour. Leave the other half of the puree and the extra bubbly for that second glass!

TONIGHT'S FORECAST:

99 per cent chance of

BUBBLES

IN WINE THERE IS

TRUTH.

PROVERB

WINE IS ONE OF THE
MOST CIVILISED THINGS
IN THE WORLD.

ERNEST HEMINGWAY

PROSECCO ALERT!

The global consumption of Prosecco has more than doubled in recent years.

According to the International Wine and Spirit Research Company, Italy is the only country that beats the UK in Prosecco consumption.

CRANBERRY AND PROSECCO FIZZ

SERVES 4

Great for the festive season or
any winter celebration. Otherwise,
just have one because they're
delicious and you deserve it!

INGREDIENTS

- 4 tbsp orange liqueur (e.g. Grand Marnier)

- 4 tbsp cranberry juice

- 1 bottle chilled Prosecco

- 12 fresh cranberries

- 4 rosemary sprigs

METHOD

- Add one tablespoon of the orange liqueur, one tablespoon of the cranberry juice and three cranberries to four chilled champagne flutes. Fill with Prosecco, garnish with the rosemary sprigs and serve.

Tick, tock, it's
PROSECCO
O'CLOCK

WINE
IS LIFE.

PETRONIUS

BLACK VELVET

SERVES 4

A barman at Brooks's Club in London first created the drink in 1861 to mourn the death of Prince Albert, Queen Victoria's husband. It is supposed to symbolise the black or purple cloth armbands worn by mourners.

INGREDIENTS

- 2 cans Guinness
- 1 bottle chilled Prosecco

METHOD

- Half fill four champagne flutes with Guinness, then slowly top them up with chilled Prosecco.

I COOK
WITH WINE.
SOMETIMES I
EVEN ADD IT TO
THE FOOD.

W. C. FIELDS

'TRUST ME,
YOU CAN
DANCE.'
— Prosecco

ALCOHOL IS NOT THE

ANSWER;

IT JUST MAKES YOU

FORGET THE

QUESTION.

ANONYMOUS

I ONLY DRINK ON
TWO OCCASIONS –
WHEN I'M THIRSTY
AND WHEN I'M NOT.

BRENDAN BEHAN

APEROL SPRITZ

SERVES 1

Aperol Spritz became popular in the 1950s and is now considered to be Italy's drink (after Prosecco, that is!). This low-alcohol cocktail is built around Aperol, a semi-sweet, slightly bitter aperitif from northern Italy.

INGREDIENTS

- 3 parts Prosecco
- 2 parts Aperol
- Splash of soda water
- Orange slice for garnish

METHOD

- Add the Prosecco to a tumbler with plenty of ice.

- Top with the Aperol and soda water.

- Add a slice of orange and serve.

Sip, sip,
HOORAY!

A MAN WILL
BE ELOQUENT IF
YOU GIVE HIM
GOOD WINE.

RALPH WALDO EMERSON

CLASSIC
PROSECCO COCKTAIL

SERVES 1

A great festive treat that simply replaces the famous French fizz with the Italian one.

INGREDIENTS

* 1 white sugar cube
* 2 dashes Angostura bitters
* 20 ml cognac
* Enough chilled Prosecco to fill the glass

METHOD

- Place the sugar cube onto a spoon and add the bitters.

- Drop the soaked sugar cube into a chilled champagne flute and add the cognac.

- Top up the glass with Prosecco and serve.

NOW IS THE TIME
FOR DRINKING,
NOW THE TIME
TO DANCE
FOOTLOOSE
UPON THE EARTH.

HORACE

FERMENTATION EQUALS EQUALS CIVILISATION.

JOHN CIARDI

PROSECCO ALERT!

A small glass of Prosecco has only slightly more calories than a chocolate digestive biscuit.

PROSECCO COBBLER

SERVES 1

This cocktail first emerged in America in the 1930s and was originally made with sherry. Today, all sorts of variations are used, including this delicious Prosecco one.

INGREDIENTS

* ½ tsp lemon juice
* ½ tsp curaçao
* Slice of orange
* Enough chilled Prosecco to fill the glass

METHOD

- Half fill a goblet glass with crushed ice.
- Add the lemon juice, curaçao and orange slice.
- Stir, top up with Prosecco, stir again and serve.

WINE IS BOTTLED POETRY.

ROBERT LOUIS STEVENSON

WINE IS A

PASSPORT

TO THE

WORLD.

THOM ELKJER

D'ARTAGNAN

SERVES 1

Named after d'Artagnan, the fourth musketeer, this drink is a celebration of chivalry and friendship.

INGREDIENTS

- 1 tsp Armagnac
- 1 tsp orange liqueur (e.g. Grand Marnier)
- 3 tsp chilled orange juice
- ½ tsp simple sugar syrup
- Slice of orange
- Enough chilled Prosecco to fill the glass

METHOD

- Pour all the ingredients, apart from the Prosecco, into a chilled champagne flute.

- Stir gently, then top up with Prosecco and garnish with an orange twist.

I MAY
NOT SPEAK
ITALIAN, BUT
I'M FLUENT
in Prosecco

A HANGOVER IS THE
WRATH OF GRAPES.

DOROTHY PARKER

A BOTTLE OF WINE
CONTAINS MORE
PHILOSOPHY THAN
ALL THE BOOKS
IN THE WORLD.

LOUIS PASTEUR

Never too
BUSY FOR
FIZZY

PROSECCO CHOCOLATE POTS

SERVES 4

Prosecco and chocolate –
what more could you ask for?!

INGREDIENTS

- 135 ml double cream
- 150 g dark chocolate, finely chopped
- ¾ tsp light muscovado sugar
- 60 ml Prosecco
- 15 g unsalted butter, cut into small pieces
- Whipped cream, to serve

METHOD

- Heat the cream and sugar over a medium heat and keep stirring until the sugar has dissolved and the cream is just about to boil.

- Meanwhile, put the chocolate and butter into a heatproof bowl.

- Pour the cream over the chocolate and butter, then stir until the chocolate has melted and the mixture is smooth.

- Stir in the Prosecco.

- Pour into four small espresso cups and place in the fridge to set (about 4–5 hours).

- Take out of the fridge about 30 minutes before serving and top with whipped cream.

OH NO,
I bought
PROSECCO
INSTEAD
of milk
AGAIN...

ALCOHOL

MAY NOT SOLVE
YOUR PROBLEMS,
BUT NEITHER WILL

WATER
OR MILK.

ANONYMOUS

GIN, ELDERFLOWER AND PROSECCO COCKTAIL

SERVES 4

Although this cocktail is
like summer in a glass, it can be
enjoyed all year round.

INGREDIENTS

- 80 ml gin
- Elderflower cordial (a dash in each glass)
- 1 bottle chilled Prosecco
- Fresh mint sprigs and/or cucumber slices

METHOD

- Pour a dash of elderflower cordial and 20 ml of gin into each Martini or wine glass and simply top up with cold Prosecco. Decorate with a sprig of fresh mint or slice of cucumber, if you wish.

WINE AND FRIENDS ARE A GREAT BLEND.

ERNEST HEMINGWAY

ONE
PROSECCO,
TWO
PROSECCO,
THREE
PROSECCO,
Floor!

BUCK'S FIZZ

SERVES 4

Traditionally served on
Christmas morning or at a
pre-wedding breakfast.

INGREDIENTS

* 1 bottle chilled Prosecco
* Large carton orange juice

METHOD

* In four chilled champagne flutes, mix two parts
  of Prosecco with one part of orange juice.

A BOTTLE OF WINE
BEGS TO BE SHARED;
I HAVE NEVER MET A
MISERLY WINE LOVER.

CLIFTON FADIMAN

GOOD WINE IS
A GOOD FAMILIAR
CREATURE, IF IT
BE WELL USED.

WILLIAM SHAKESPEARE

GOOD THINGS HAPPEN TO THOSE WHO

drink bubbly

FRENCH 75

SERVES 4

The kick of the alcohol in this Parisian cocktail is said to have felt like being shelled by the French 75-mm field gun used in World War One. (It is traditionally made with champagne, but this is a great Italian alternative!)

INGREDIENTS

* 120 ml gin
* 1 bottle chilled Prosecco
* 60 ml freshly squeezed lemon juice
* Icing sugar
* Crushed ice
* Lemon twist to garnish

METHOD

- Mix the gin, lemon juice and sugar together.

- Divide the mix between four flutes containing crushed ice, then fill to the top with Prosecco. Garnish with a twist of lemon.

FROM WINE WHAT SUDDEN FRIENDSHIP SPRINGS!

JOHN GAY

WINE CHEERS
THE SAD, REVIVES
THE OLD,
INSPIRES THE
YOUNG, MAKES
WEARINESS
FORGET HIS TOIL.

LORD BYRON

WATERMELON PROSECCO COCKTAIL

SERVES 6–8

Serve in jam-jar glasses for the
perfect summer party drink.

INGREDIENTS

- 1 watermelon
- 200 ml vodka
- 1 bottle chilled Prosecco
- Fresh mint

METHOD

- Peel, then chop the watermelon into chunks and pop them into the freezer, along with your bottle of vodka.

- When you're ready to serve, put about a quarter of the watermelon chunks into a blender along with the vodka and blitz until smooth. Top up with Prosecco and then blend on a low setting to combine.

- Fill a large pitcher with ice, pour the pink cocktail over it and garnish with plenty of fresh mint leaves.

POP
fizz
CLINK

WHEN I READ ABOUT
THE EVILS OF
DRINKING,
I GAVE UP
READING.

HENNY YOUNGMAN

HEALTH IS WHAT MY
FRIENDS ARE ALWAYS
DRINKING TO BEFORE
THEY FALL DOWN.

PHYLLIS DILLER

WINE ADDS
A SMILE TO
FRIENDSHIP AND
A SPARK TO LOVE.

EDMONDO DE AMICIS

RASPBERRY PROSECCO COCKTAIL

SERVES 1

A delicious variation
of the Kir Royale.

INGREDIENTS

* 2–4 raspberries
* 1 tsp raspberry liqueur
* Enough chilled Prosecco to fill the glass

METHOD

* Drop the raspberries in a chilled flute and add the raspberry liqueur.
* Top with Prosecco and serve.

I'LL BE
THERE IN A
Prosecco!

PROSECCO ALERT!

Prosecco wasn't bubbly until the nineteenth century. The version we know today was first produced by Carpenè Malvolti winery.

JUST THE
SIMPLE ACT OF
TASTING A GLASS
OF WINE IS ITS
OWN EVENT.

DAVID HYDE PIERCE

SLOE GIN AND BLACKBERRY SPARKLE

SERVES 1

Gin and Prosecco make
the best of friends.

INGREDIENTS

- 30 ml sloe gin
- Blackberries
- Enough chilled Prosecco to fill the glass

METHOD

- Add the sloe gin to a tumbler along with a blackberry or two before topping it up with Prosecco.

ALCOHOL, TAKEN IN SUFFICIENT QUANTITIES, MAY PRODUCE ALL THE EFFECTS OF DRUNKENNESS.

OSCAR WILDE

WINE TO ME IS PASSION... WINE IS ART. IT'S CULTURE. IT'S THE ESSENCE OF CIVILISATION AND THE ART OF LIVING.

ROBERT MONDAVI

DRINK
MORE
~~water~~
PROSECCO

CHERRY AND AMARETTO FIZZ

SERVES 1

Decadence at its booziest!

INGREDIENTS

* 1 cherry
* 1 tbsp kirsch
* 1 part amaretto
* 3 parts chilled Prosecco

METHOD

* Place the cherry and kirsch in the bottom of a flute.
* Top with the amaretto and Prosecco.

ALL YOU NEED
is love and
PROSECCO

WHEN A RECIPE SAYS
'ADD WINE', NEVER
ASK 'TO WHAT?'

ANONYMOUS

SOBER OR BLOTTO, THIS IS
YOUR MOTTO: KEEP

MUDDLING
THROUGH.

P. G. WODEHOUSE

SHERBET CITRUS FIZZ

SERVES 1

Let the taste buds be tantalised!

INGREDIENTS

* 1 heaped tsp lemon sorbet
* A few drops of lime cordial
* Enough chilled Prosecco to fill the glass
* Slice of lemon

METHOD

* Into the bottom of a tall flute, add the lemon sorbet.
* Add a dash of lime cordial and top with Prosecco.
* Stir quickly but carefully before garnishing with the lemon slice.

ALL WINES SHOULD BE
TASTED; SOME SHOULD
ONLY BE SIPPED, BUT
WITH OTHERS, DRINK
THE WHOLE BOTTLE.

PAULO COELHO

SOMETIMES TOO MUCH TO DRINK IS BARELY ENOUGH.

MARK TWAIN

LAUGHTER
IS THE BEST
MEDICINE...
if you can't find the Prosecco

SUMMER COCKTAIL

SERVES 1

Sit back, relax and watch the sun set
with your fizzy friend in hand.

INGREDIENTS

* 15 ml vodka
* 15 ml raspberry liqueur
* 30 ml pineapple juice
* Enough chilled Prosecco to fill the glass
* 1 raspberry

METHOD

* Pour everything into a wine glass and give it
  a very gentle stir.
* Pop in the raspberry.

I DRINK WHEN I HAVE OCCASION, AND SOMETIMES WHEN I HAVE NO OCCASION.

MIGUEL DE CERVANTES

THE JUICE OF

THE GRAPE

IS THE LIQUID QUINTESSENCE

OF CONCENTRATED

SUNBEAMS.

THOMAS LOVE PEACOCK

PROSECCO is the ANSWER. WHAT was the QUESTION?

PEACHY PROSECCO COCKTAIL

SERVES 1

The subtle flavour of
peaches will bring out the sharper
notes in your Prosecco.

INGREDIENTS

- 15 ml vodka
- 15 ml peach liqueur
- 15 ml amaretto
- 30 ml orange juice
- Squeeze of fresh lemon juice
- Enough Prosecco to fill the glass

- 1 basil leaf
- Fresh peach slice

METHOD

- Add all of the ingredients, except the Prosecco and peach slice, to a shaker filled with ice.

- Shake well and pour into a tumbler.

- Top the glass with Prosecco and garnish with the peach slice.

IF FOOD IS THE BODY
OF GOOD LIVING,
WINE IS ITS SOUL.

CLIFTON FADIMAN

REALITY IS
AN ILLUSION
CREATED BY A LACK
OF ALCOHOL.

N. F. SIMPSON

LIMONCELLO AND PROSECCO JELLY

SERVES 4

Limoncello is another
Italian drink that works well
with the popular Prosecco.

INGREDIENTS

* 5 gelatine leaves
* 350 ml Prosecco
* 1 tbsp caster sugar
* 6 tbsp limoncello
* Edible gold glitter

METHOD

- Put the gelatine leaves in a bowl of cold water for 5 minutes or until soft.

- Squeeze the leaves and discard the water.

- Put the limoncello into a heatproof bowl that fits over a pan of boiling water, add the gelatine and sugar, and heat until gently dissolved.

- Remove from the heat and allow to cool slightly, then pour the syrup into a pitcher along with the Prosecco and stir.

- Very slowly pour the jelly mix into four Martini glasses until each glass is almost full. Refrigerate for a couple of hours until set.

- Top with gold glitter to serve.

Keep calm
AND DRINK
PROSECCO

WINE IS A LIVING LIQUID CONTAINING NO PRESERVATIVES.

JULIA CHILD

WINE MAKES
DAILY LIVING
EASIER, LESS
HURRIED, WITH
FEWER TENSIONS
AND MORE
TOLERANCE.

BENJAMIN FRANKLIN

WINE BRINGS

TO LIGHT

THE HIDDEN SECRETS OF

THE SOUL.

HORACE

RHUBARB BELLINI

SERVES 6

A delicious alternative to the classic Bellini using rhubarb instead of peach.

INGREDIENTS

- 300 g rhubarb, trimmed and finely chopped
- 75 g sugar
- 1 bottle of chilled Prosecco

METHOD

- Put the rhubarb and sugar in a pan with two tablespoons of water.
- Cover with a lid, bring to the boil and simmer for 2 minutes.

- Remove the lid and allow to simmer for a few more minutes, stirring occasionally.

- Once the mixture is of a thick, compote consistency, take it off the heat and whizz it into a puree with a hand blender or food processor.

- Allow to cool.

- Spoon the mixture evenly into chilled champagne flutes and top with Prosecco to serve.

I ONLY DRINK
PROSECCO ON
TWO OCCASIONS:

when it's my
birthday and
when it's not

PROSECCO ALERT!

A cork can travel up to 25 mph when popping out of a bottle, so look out!

STRAWBERRY AND PROSECCO FLOAT

SERVES 4

After this, you'll be feeling sweet, fizzy and a little bit dizzy!

INGREDIENTS

- 340 g strawberries, quartered
- 1 tbsp sugar
- 600 ml quality vanilla ice cream
- 1 bottle chilled Prosecco

METHOD

- Toss the strawberries in the sugar and leave for 30 minutes.

- Add one scoop of vanilla ice cream each to four wine glasses.

- Divide the sugar-coated strawberries between the glasses.

- Fill the glasses with Prosecco and serve with a spoon and a straw.

BUT I'M NOT
SO THINK AS YOU
DRUNK I AM.

J. C. SQUIRE

THE BEST WINES ARE THE ONES WE DRINK WITH FRIENDS.

ANONYMOUS

MIMOSA

SERVES 8

A perfect brunch cocktail that's simple and quick to make.

INGREDIENTS

- 750 ml chilled orange juice (freshly squeezed is best)
- 120 ml orange liqueur
- 1 bottle chilled Prosecco

METHOD

- Fill champagne flutes with one part chilled Prosecco, one part orange juice and one part orange liqueur.
- No need to stir as the cocktail will mix together on its own.

I ONLY
drink
PROSECCO
ON DAYS
ending
IN 'Y'

DRINK IS
THE FEAST OF
REASON AND
THE FLOW
OF SOUL.

ALEXANDER POPE

EITHER GIVE
ME MORE WINE
OR LEAVE
ME ALONE.

RUMI

SPICED PEAR PROSECCO

SERVES 1

The perfect drink to warm your
cockles on a crisp winter's day.

INGREDIENTS

* 1 tbsp caster sugar
* ½ tsp ground cinnamon
* 1 tbsp ginger syrup
* Equal quantities of pear juice
  and Prosecco to fill the glass
* Slice of stem ginger, to garnish

METHOD

- Dip the rim of a champagne flute into water and then into a dish of caster sugar mixed with ground cinnamon.

- Add the ginger syrup and top with both the pear juice and Prosecco.

- Garnish with the slice of stem ginger.

Espresso
THEN
PROSECCO

WINE IS

MORE THAN A

BEVERAGE

- IT'S A

LIFESTYLE.

ANONYMOUS

GINGER AND LIME SPARKLER

SERVES 1

A concoction of health and hedonism.

INGREDIENTS

* 25 ml ginger syrup
* 1 lime
* Enough chilled Prosecco to fill the glass

METHOD

* Pour the ginger syrup into a flute and add the juice of half a lime.
* Top up with Prosecco and stir briefly.
* Garnish with half a slim slice of lime.

THE PROBLEM WITH THE WORLD IS THAT EVERYONE IS A FEW DRINKS BEHIND.

HUMPHREY BOGART

FRIENDS DON'T LET FRIENDS

drink Prosecco on their own

I KNEW I WAS DRUNK.
I FELT SOPHISTICATED
AND COULDN'T
PRONOUNCE IT.

ANONYMOUS

MAPLE FIZZ

SERVES 1

The sweetness of the maple syrup works well with the tang of cranberry.

INGREDIENTS

- 2 tsp maple syrup
- 50 ml chilled cranberry juice
- 100 ml chilled Prosecco

METHOD

- Shake the maple syrup and cranberry juice over ice in a cocktail shaker.
- Strain into a tumbler and top with Prosecco.
- Stir quickly before serving.

WINE FILLS THE
HEART WITH
COURAGE.

PLATO

THIS HOUSE RUNS ON
love, laughter
AND
PROSECCO

A CONSTANT PROOF
THAT GOD
LOVES US,
AND LOVES TO SEE US
HAPPY.

BENJAMIN FRANKLIN ON WINE

CHRISTMAS COCKTAIL

SERVES 1

A great way to refresh after all that
Christmas food!

INGREDIENTS

* 15 ml Campari
* 30 ml fresh grapefruit juice
* Enough extra-dry Prosecco to fill the glass
* Grapefruit peel

METHOD

- In an ice-filled cocktail shaker, add the Campari, grapefruit juice and Prosecco.

- Shake until well combined.

- Strain into your Martini glass.

- Rub the grapefruit peel along the rim and add it to the glass.

Monday:
IT'S NOTHING
PROSECCO
can't fix

PROSECCO ALERT!

Over 60 per cent of all Prosecco is now produced outside its traditional regions of north-eastern Italy, and this figure is continually rising as demand increases.

DARK CHOCOLATE PROSECCO TRUFFLES

MAKES 20–22

So moreish, it won't take long
to eat them all.

INGREDIENTS

- 200 g dark chocolate, chopped
- 75 ml double cream
- 3 tbsp Prosecco
- 1 tsp grated orange zest
- Cocoa powder for coating

METHOD

- Melt the dark chocolate and cream together in a basin over a bain-marie, stirring occasionally.

- Once melted, add the orange zest and Prosecco.

- Cool to room temperature or leave overnight in the fridge.

- Scoop small balls with a melon scoop and roll in cocoa powder.

- Store the truffles in an airtight container and keep refrigerated. They will last for up to a week.

IF WE SIP
THE WINE, WE
FIND DREAMS
COMING UPON
US OUT OF THE
IMMINENT NIGHT.

D. H. LAWRENCE

PROSECCO MADE ME

do it

PROSECCO ROYALE

SERVES 1

A cocktail for kings and queens –
yes, that's you!

INGREDIENTS

* 1 part crème de cassis
* 3 parts Prosecco
* 1 tbsp lemon juice
* 2 blueberries
* 1 sprig of thyme

METHOD

* Gently stir together the crème de cassis, lemon juice and Prosecco.

* Skewer a couple of blueberries onto a sprig of thyme and pop it into the glass to serve.

ABSTAINER: A WEAK
PERSON WHO YIELDS
TO THE TEMPTATION
OF DENYING HIMSELF
A PLEASURE.

AMBROSE BIERCE

PROSECCO PUNCH

SERVES 4

Ideal for when you're hosting
a party or gathering.

INGREDIENTS

- 1 lemon, thinly sliced
- 2 tbsp sugar
- 10–15 strawberries, hulled and sliced
- 1 bottle of Prosecco

METHOD

- Place the sliced lemon in the bottom of a punch bowl.
- Sprinkle the sugar on top and muddle.
- Add the sliced strawberries.
- Muddle (crush) the strawberries into the lemon.
- Add the Prosecco to the bowl.
- Fill with ice and serve.

FOR WHEN THE WINE
IS IN, THE WIT IS OUT.

THOMAS BECON

TIME TO
drink
PROSECCO
AND DANCE
on the
TABLE

WINE IS JUST A CONVERSATION WAITING TO HAPPEN.

JESSICA ALTIERI

THE CONNOISSEUR DOES NOT DRINK WINE BUT TASTES ITS SECRETS.

SALVADOR DALÍ

AUTUMN COCKTAIL

SERVES 1

Perfect for when you've just returned home from a day of leaf-crunching and conker-collecting.

INGREDIENTS

- 100 ml Prosecco
- 4 blackberries
- 30 ml vodka
- Dash of fresh orange juice
- Dash of simple sugar syrup
- Splash of orange liqueur

METHOD

- Pour the Prosecco into a Collins glass.

- Muddle (crush) three blackberries in a cocktail shaker and then add the vodka, orange juice, orange liqueur and some ice.

- Shake vigorously and then strain into the glass.

- Garnish with the remaining blackberry.

BUT FIRST, PROSECCO!

WINE IS EARTH'S

ANSWER

TO THE

SUN.

MARGARET FULLER

STRAWBERRY AND PEACH BELLINI

SERVES 1

An even fruitier take on
the classic Bellini recipe.

INGREDIENTS

- 400 g strawberries, hulled
- 25 ml peach schnapps
- Enough Prosecco to fill the glass

METHOD

- Place the strawberries into a container and put them in the freezer.

- Once the strawberries are frozen, place four into a champagne flute.

- Pour in the peach schnapps and then fill the flute to the top with Prosecco.

FEELING FIZZY AND fabulous

WINE CAN BE A BETTER
TEACHER THAN INK.

STEPHEN FRY

CHERRY POP PROSECCO COCKTAIL

SERVES 4

The drink that has everything,
plus the cherry on top.

INGREDIENTS

- 15 ml gin
- 15 ml cherry brandy
- 10 ml lemon juice
- 4 cherries
- A bottle of Prosecco

METHOD

- Pour the gin, brandy, lemon juice and a little ice into a cocktail shaker.

- Shake and strain into flutes.

- Top up the glasses with Prosecco and garnish with a cherry.

If you're interested in finding out more about our books, find us on Facebook at Summersdale Publishers and follow us on Twitter at @Summersdale.

www.summersdale.com

Image credits

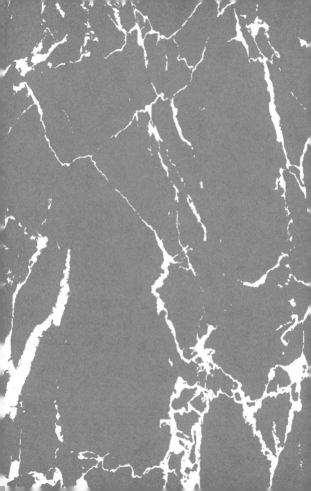

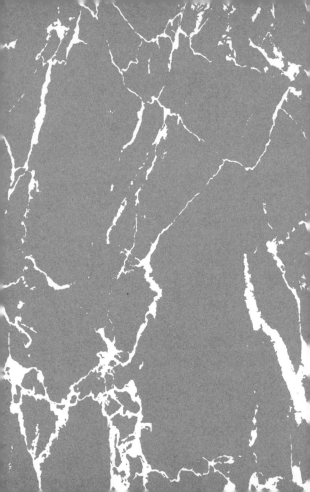